KV-512-366

'he

HQ

19 JUL 2005

11 JUL 2006

−5 DEC 2006

17 APR 2007

−5 JUN 2007

−7 APR 2008

25 AUG 2009

HQ

2 5 JUL 2011

− 4 OCT 2013

11 MAR 2014

2 1 AUG 2014
2 8 OCT 2014

01 DEC 2015

2 6 MAR 2016

14 JUN 2019

20 JUL 2019

06 JAN 2019

20 MAR 2020

16 MAY 2022

18 JUL 2022

03 SEP 2022

3 1 OCT 2022

2 0 FEB 2023

ABERDEENSHIRE LIBRARY
AND INFORMATION SERVICE 2 4 APR 2023

MELD Kendell, Patric   IM

Polar bears /   1 7 JUN 2023
Patricia
Kendell
             J599.
             786
1576054

A L I S
1576054

Polar Bears

Patricia Kendell

HODDER
Wayland

An imprint of Hodder Children's Books

Chimpanzees   Dolphins   Elephants
Lions   Polar Bears   Tigers

 © 2002 White-Thomson Publishing Ltd

Produced for Hodder Wayland by White-Thomson Publishing Ltd

Editor: Kay Barnham
Designer: Tim Mayer
Consultant: Peter Prokosch is the founder and coor
  WWF International Arctic Programme.
Language Consultant: Norah Granger, Senior Lectu
  Education at the University of Brighton
Picture research: Shelley Noronha – Glass Onion F

Published in Great Britain in 2002 by Hodder Way
an imprint of Hodder Children's Books.

The right of Patricia Kendell to be identified as the author of this
Work has been asserted by her in accordance with the Copyright,
Designs and Patents Act 1988.

Photograph acknowledgements:
B & C Alexander: 1, 21;
Bruce Coleman: 3 (third), 8, 25 (Fred Bruemmer), 26 (Johnny
Johnson);
FLPA: 11 (L Accusani), 15 (E & D Hosking), 3 (fourth), 10, 16
(Minden Pictures), 3 (first), 5, 14 (Mark Newman), 6, 17 (Fritz
Polking), 22 (E Pott/Sunset), 4, 7 (Silvestris), 12 (Roger Tidman);
Oxford Scientific Films: 3 (second), 18, 19 (Daniel J Cox), 27
(Richard Kolar), 29 (Hans Reinhard), 9 (Norbert Rosing);
Staffan Widstrand: 13, 23, 28;
Still Pictures: 20, 32 (Fred Bruemmer);
HWPL: 24.

Kendell, Patrici

Polar bears /
Patricia Kendell

J599.
786

11576054

All instructions, information and advice given in this book are
believed to be reliable and accurate. All guidelines and warnings
should be read carefully and the author, packager, editor and
publisher cannot accept responsibility for injuries or damage arising
out of failure to comply with the same.

. No part of this publication may be reproduced,
l system, or transmitted, in any form or by any
  prior written permission of the publisher, nor be
d in any form of binding or cover other than
  published and without a similar condition being
  sequent purchaser.

aloguing in Publication Data
Kendell, Patricia
  Polar bear. - (In the wild)
  1. Polar bear
  I. Title
  599.7'86

ISBN: 0 7502 3827 5

Printed and bound in Italy by G. Canale C.S.p.A. Turin

Hodder Children's Books
A division of Hodder Headline Limited
338 Euston Road, London NW1 3BH

Produced in association with WWF-UK.
WWF-UK registered charity number 1081247.
A company limited by guarantee number 4016725.
Panda device © 1986 WWF ® WWF registered trademark owner.

They break into seal dens and feast on seal pups like this one.

Summer Food

In warmer weather, the **pack ice** melts. Polar bears have to find other food on land. The hungry bears eat birds' eggs, grass and berries to survive.

This cub has found some seaweed to eat.

Growing up

Cubs leave their mothers when they are about two and a half years old. They **roam** over the ice looking for enough food to survive.

18

They leap from **ice floe** to ice floe looking for fish and seals.

Meeting other bears

When winter comes, polar bears gather together,
waiting for the ice to become strong enough to walk on.

Some polar bears have fun while they wait.
These bears are just playing at fighting.

Finding a mate

This polar bear is sniffing the spring air. It is now time to start a new family.

This male bear is looking for a **mate**.

Threats...

Leaks from oil tankers can **pollute** the sea. Polar bears are also threatened when **poisonous chemicals** wash from the land into the sea.

This polar bear has been put to sleep for a short time
so scientists can see how much poison is in its blood.

...and dangers

The Earth is becoming warmer and the polar ice is melting earlier each year. Less ice means fewer seal pups for polar bears to eat.

These hungry polar bears are looking for food
near a town. There is a danger that frightened
people will kill them.

Helping polar bears to survive

Some polar bears now live in special **reserves** where they are safe. People watch the polar bears and find out more about their way of life.

The more we learn about polar bears, the more
we can help them to survive in the future.

Further information

Find out more about how we can help polar bears in the future.

ORGANIZATIONS TO CONTACT

WWF-UK
Panda House, Weyside Park,
Godalming, Surrey GU7 1XR
Tel: 01483 426444

Care for the Wild International
1 Ashfolds, Horsham Road,
Rusper, West Sussex RH12 4QX
Tel: 01293 871596

BOOKS

Will there be polar bears?: Julia Jarman
(Picture book) Little Mammoth 1993

The last polar bears: Harry Horse
(Picture book) Viking 2000

For more fluent readers
Polar Bears – facts, stories and activities:
Lucy Baker, Franklin Watts 1990

The polar bear: Caroline Brett (Junior
Survival library) BoxTree 1990

Glossary

WEBSITES

Most young children will need adult help when visiting websites. Those below have child-friendly pages that can be bookmarked.

WWF Virtual wildlife
www.panda.org/kids/wildlife

WWF's virtual wildlife pages.

Polar Bears Alive
www.polarbearsalive.org
The Polar Bear Gallery page contains photographs children will find interesting.

Visit learn.co.uk for more resources.

It should be noted that a polar bear's natural habitat is sea ice, but this is a very difficult place to take photographs. As they spend some time on land, this is where most of the photographs in this book have been taken.

Arctic – the area around the North Pole where it is very cold and icy. This includes the northern parts of Russia and North America.

ice floe – large area of frozen sea.

mate – male or female partner. They make babies together.

pack ice – solid ice covering the sea.

poisonous chemicals – chemicals that harm the environment.

pollute – to spoil with harmful chemicals or gases.

reserves – safe places where wild animals can live freely.

roam – to wander about.

Index